DADDY, IS JAMES A NIGGER?

Is Racism Nature or Nurture?

CAROL R . ELLIS

CONTENTS

Foreword

The use of the word nigger in the title of this book is not meant to be racially denigrating; its use is a matter of face. The word nigger belongs to no race or ethnic group, its entitlement does not belong to African-Americans more than any other group. For African-Americans who feel entitled to use the term in language and music I would say substitute the term inferior person every time you want to use the word nigger and then you will understand what is conveyed by the term nigger. For whites, or any other ethnic group to use the word nigger is despicable, but for blacks to use the word nigger is psychologically self-genocidal. It is the ultimate put-down; it has no artistic, literary, intellectual or social merit. It is not fair to burden young black children with the notion they were born inferior because they are anything but. Young black girls should not be shown sex stereotypes and young black boys should not be limited by stereotypical depictions of black males as thugs. Like all children they are beautiful and full of promise and that is what they should hear.

This book seeks to raise the question whether racism is born of nature or whether it is, in fact, learned from a racist family, or community, environment, which, either knowingly or unknowingly, nurtures the roots of discrimination in the formative young minds of children. The intent of this book is to enable individuals who seek awareness to search deep within themselves to discover whether they feel racism, where it came from, how it manifests itself in their own behavior, and how it affects what they may be teaching their children by their action, words, or more subtle forms of communication. One subtle form of communicating a racist attitude is to lock the car doors when the car stops for a traffic light near a group of young black males. Another nonverbal racist communication is to cross the street when several black males approaching.

There are families who are decidedly nonracist and may have children who conform to the nonracist way of thinking only to find they have one child who decides on his/her own that it just does not like people of other races, religions, or cultures. It seems no amount of discussion can keep the child from being a racist, and the attitude is a puzzlement which cannot be easily explained.

There are racist families whose children decide that racism is hard to understand or just plain wrong in the first place. A very young child is capable of noticing differences in people, most notable their color. Left to their own devices, children may be very accepting of children of other races, especially if they are of the same size and age. If questions arise from young children, they are often extremely sensitive as to how they are answered. The answer to an innocent question on the part of a child about color differences can profoundly affect how they subsequently build their own attitudes about others. Parents, as well as extended family and friends who do have racist feelings, even if they do not recognize or admit they do, may ever so subtly impart an attitude of racism in the mind of a child.

There are racists who admit they are racist and do not care what anyone thinks about them for being a racist. They do not want to change. They see no need to change. They will have to "die off" before young people in their sphere of influence can even begin to see the need for change.

Individuals and families who recognize racism, and the negative environment that it creates for them and their children, do seek to be a part of the solution. The consequences of racism in our evolving social, educational, political, and economic environment are monumental. Just as we face environmental pollution in our atmosphere, we also experience the pollution of the soul from racism. Racism by African-Americans is just as damning as racism by European-Americans and is equally detrimental to their children in their journey for economic and social justice. Racial discrimination in all forms contributes to the destruction of economic advancement for everyone regardless of one's own ethnicity.

Dedication

To the memory of James and Mattie who lived out their lives in Virginia's segregated South at a time when they were not free to go where they may have wanted to go and to do things they may have wanted to do just because of the color of their skin.

To the memory of my father who was never able to overcome his racial bigotry despite his affection for his good friend James who was black. This writing in no way is meant to vilify him for his racial attitude. He lived his life to the very best of his ability, and I appreciate the struggle he had, crying to raise a family with only a child third-grade education and poverty as a constant companion in life. He was never able to answer my questions because he did not know the answers. Since he has passed on now, I cannot discuss his racist attitudes with the understanding I have acquired over the years about why he and others ever held such beliefs. I can only move forward and hope to make a difference by working for social justice.

Acknowledgments

With gratitude and humility, I want to thank my wonderful husband, Sandy, for his patience, encouragement, and loving support during the process of writing this book. He helped to rein in some of my stronger statements and soften the impact of what may have otherwise been a bit too direct. He is the one who has been steadfast in the assertion that I should write. I am not sure this particular book is what he had in mind.

Introduction

This book is about growing up as a poor white girl on a farm in the "segregated South" in the 1950s and '60s. I do not know if we were "po' white trash" or nor, but if we were not, we must nor have been far from it. The true stories recount memories of my youth, mostly aged three to six years old, before going to school. Some of the stories take place as late as my teens. It is a retrospective view of the events, people, and places that formed my earliest recollections about racial differences through actual experiences.

The question, "Daddy, is James a nigger?" is one that I actually asked my father. The question itself, not particularly remarkable coming from a four-year-old kid, was nor the issue. The issue rested with the "conflicting" feelings that were generated because of the duplicitous answer braced with the hypocrisy that even a chinking child could detect. The uneasy feelings remained weighted in my psyche, the mental equivalent of the famed albatross around the mariner's neck, chat caused me to continue to question the source of society's, and specifically my, prejudice regarding any and all manner of people.

Questions, questions, and more questions! I have always been accused of asking too many questions. Even if was told to stop asking so many questions, the questions were still in my head, rattling around, restless, and pondering-a mental racket that would not go away.

I thought, as a teenager in the 1960s, that if all of us were "peeled like a grape," who would judge our ethnicity? How would judgments about intelligence be determined? Who would we be afraid of? Who would be considered inferior? Why on earth would anyone consider Martin Luther King inferior? As I watched the civil rights movement play out on television. I thought he was a very brave leader. I cried when he was assassinated. I thought a lot about his, wife, children, and what they must have had to endure because of his demands for racial equality and social justice. Why could not all kids attend the schools closest to them? Why did some white people, like my father think the way they did? Why did some people seem to have a label, like guinea, spic, wap, white trash, nigger, nigra, biggety niggas, colored, jigaboo, pickaninny, coons, HiYella, Chinks, Japs and on and on?

I remember the first black girl who came to my high school about 10 years after the mandate for integration in Brown vs Board of Education. She seemed so alone and stood out even in large gatherings. I did not go out of my way to approach her; no whites did. She was pointed at and whispered about, and called "out token nigger." I felt miserable for her but not enough, I suppose, to befriend her. I know I did not think of her as a "nigger," that is for sure. I thought she was awfully brave, and I could not help but wonder how I would feel I were suddenly placed in all-black school. It was beyond my comprehension to think of myself alone in an all-black school. Reflecting on my inaction, in retrospect, makes me feel sick; but I had enough trouble trying to fit in myself without taking on someone else's issues. Our family was poor; and there was no way to get involved in after-school activities like cheerleading, band or athletics because I had no transportation except to hitchhike. I hitched frequently and thought little about any risk involved. It was just a way to get where I needed to go. "Poor" was a label as powerful as "black" and caused just as much unjust isolation, or so I thought.

Note*
The stories in this book do not necessarily follow strictly in chronological order. In some cases, there may be stories in which events may have occurred later and appear before stories that happened earlier because it was necessary to make a particular point.

Biographical Sketch

I was born Carol Robertson in 1949 at the University of Virginia Hospital in Charlottesville, Virginia, and lived my early childhood in Nelson County, Virginia, on the farm which is the site of my early explorations into racial and all other forms of life experiences. It follows that my life would be more than a little turbulent when my mother told my father that I was on the way because her water had broken, and my father told her to go back to sleep; she had just wet the bed. According to my mother's account, what ensued was a very fast, very bumpy ride down mostly dirt roads, thirty-five miles to the university hospital where I was promptly born at 5:13 a.m.

Until the time I was forced to go to school, I had been a freewheeling, independent wood nymph who had virtually no bounds except chose of Mother Nature. By today's standards of child rearing, I had an enormous amount of freedom to do anything I wanted. I went from relative to relative to visit. Mostly everyone was engaged in hard work and I never stayed long enough to get sucked into that. Everybody looked out for me, but still, there were times when no one was around for hours, and miles, so I was on my own. A huge oak tree, with a flowing canopy of large branches touching the ground, was my hideout. I had an old stump for a cable and a big limb for a chair. When I was there, I was Queen of all I surveyed. I made daisy chains and wore wild roses, thorns and all, as my jewelry. The chiggers and ticks had a feast with me around. I

collected acorns and rocks and piled chem in my castle and chose were
my riches. Cats, dogs, chickens. and squirrels were my playmates and my
subjects. I left no stone unturned in my early explorations.

I am the eldest of five children born into our family over an eighteen-
year span. At my mother's insistence, the family moved from the Nelson
Country farm to Charlottesville in 1959 to seek better economic
opportunities for my father and mother and to get a better education
for all of the children. Moving from the farm was the second time I
felt my life had ended because, as I will state later, the first was when I
had to attend school in 1955. In 1959, I was ten years old and begged
to be left with my grandparents on the farm when the family moved to
town. I hated life in town, and school in Charlottesville was no better
than school in Schuyler. I was in fights much of the time since I had not
been socialized with city children. I soon learned about boundaries to
behavior and became more accepting of others.

Though I never aspired to do so, in 1972, at the urging of my
husband, Ronny, I attended community college for two years; and later,
in 1974, I attended the University of Virginia, graduating in 1976 with
a BS degree in commerce. I majored in marketing and finance. When
first I applied to the University of Virginia, I hoped I would not be
admitted. Not only was I admitted, I was given scholarships and low-
cost student loans to attend. Prior to arriving on campus, my husband
and I had applied for low-cost, married-student housing, and we were
told there was none available. When we arrived with a very tired little
boy, and pulling a U-Haul with our 1960 Mercury, we tried one more
time to get an apartment in married student housing; sure, enough
there had just been a cancellation of a 2-bedroom unit in Copeley Hill
housing. Exhausted after the four-hour drive, we paid the necessary fees
and moved into our temporary home.

I was the first person ever, male or female, in my family to attend
college and was in one of the earliest classes at The University of Virginia
in which women were admitted to the previously all-male, state supported

school. Women had attended the university in the traditionally female fields of teaching and nursing but not business, science, or technical studies. The American Civil Liberties Union used the University of Virginia on behalf of Virginia Anne Scott and 3 other women, to allow them to attend in 1969. Though I was never told so, I believe I was the fortunate beneficiary of Affirmative Action which I still assert is the only way to achieve an equal playing field for minorities and women.

In 1974, the issue of women attending the university overlapped with the process of racial integration beginning in earnest. The first black male student was admitted to the University in 1950 under a Federal Court order but not man black students a percentage basis had been admitted. Like the turbulence in the rest of the country, it was a time of social transition; but unlike some of the rest of the country, it took place in a quiet and stately, gradual manner. After all, it was Charlottesville, Virginia, and this was the University of Virginia.

By the time I attended the University of Virginia in 1974, I had a four-year-old son, and my husband taught school in a town one hundred fifty miles south of Charlottesville to support the family and help pay tuition for my undergraduate education and our living expenses. I, and my son, lived in married-student campus housing and saw my husband on the weekends.

1974 was "the year from hell." My twelve-year-old car broke down frequently and at the most inconvenient and crucial of times. I was taking twenty credit hours. That winter, my son had strep throat, bronchitis, and pneumonia; and I missed a lot of classes. I may have been admitted to the University because of Affirmative Action, but that did not change the negative attitude of the professors and male students about women attending. The professor's cur me no slack because I had a sick child. On one occasion, I had to miss the final exam because my son was desperately ill and had a high fever. I cried to tell the professor why I missed the rest, and he told me he was "sick of excuses from brats who parried all night and were too hung over to make the test." He tried to walk away, but I followed him down the hall to the men's room; and alter his caustic comment, he slammed the men's room door in my face, and that was that. I kept pleading my case and did take the final, thanks to my advisor, which I ultimately passed. We had no money to repeat a class, so I could not fail anything. Academic achievement was the last thing on my mind; I just had to get through with passing grades, by however slim a margin.

I had to graduate as soon as possible and get a job so we would have income. I had student loans to pay back and my husband's health was getting worse. He fell down often because of multiple sclerosis and kids teased my son about his dad "being drunk." Hearing kids say mean things made us all depressed. My objective was not to try to make top grades; it was just to get out of school, period! It was a painful time, and every day was a monumental struggle; but I graduated on time, nevertheless.

My husband, who had an undergraduate degree in physics from the University of Virginia, eventually had to quit his high school teaching job because of the ravages of MS. His teaching income had been the only income we had to survive on, and our situation became even more financially tenuous. He finally joined us, and our family was reunited in Charlottesville in the fall of 1975 where he continued his work on a PhD at the University of Virginia.

Since my graduation from the University of Virginia in 1976 my husband died. I have been employed by two major corporations, worked on an MBA-ranking night classes fifty miles from where we lived while I worked a sixty-hour week-owned my own small antique business and a home staging business, and have done freelance writing in the real estate field.

A Little History

Our family farm had a history. Well, at lease an oral history. According to "oral history," the site of the farm was originally an Indian settlement along Dutch Creek in Nelson County, Virginia. The information is believed to be accurate because countless Indian artifacts were unearthed when the cornfields and vegetable gardens were tilled. My grandfather had collected quite a few of the artifacts and gave them to anyone who asked for them. They were mostly shiny white flint, and when the horse-drawn plow turned them over, the stones sparkled and gleamed in the sun. After a hard rain, they were easy to find. My grandfather believed that nothing belonged to anyone, that everything we had was just on loan while we lived, so he was generous with the artifacts and with his knowledge of them.

In rime, according to the lore, the original Indian settlement became the Bailey Plantation where slaves lived and worked. It was the slaves who allegedly placed the huge flat rocks, still there today, to construct a patio in front of the house. That is where, as a child, I made mud pies and "cooked" them in the sun.

Family oral history had it that old plantation house burned down when the family went to church one Sunday morning and left the grandmother home alone. While she was there, some embers dropped through the floor of the fireplace and caught the house on fire. She died in the flames.

Photo of Big Rocks Laid by Slaves
By: H Cowen Ellis

Prior to that time, it was also rumored that a slave had once been lashed to a post, whipped by "a mean old man," until he bled, then left out in the cold rain all night, still lashed to the post. It is believed he died of pneumonia. Even thought the house as not built by my grandfather until 1921, the "old people" said the place had the ghosts of those who had died violently while living on the property. I had no way knowing if the events repeated in the lore of the place actually happened or not, but many times, I felt an eerie unknown "presence". Heavy footsteps were heard in the house when it was known to be empty. I never felt alone as a child, I do not remember ever being afraid of the "ghosts."

If I was alone in a room of the house, I would listen; and sometimes, I would ask, "Ghost, are you in here? I never got an answer.

Meandering through the farm was an old stagecoach road (reportedly once a portion of what is now Stagebrigde Road) that ran through the property under the massive hemlocks, oaks, and American chestnut trees before the chestnut blight. Before the blight, and after, those great trees were cut to make the original tobacco barns (long since gone) and the cow and the horse barn, which is still on the property today.

The stage road had several springs where the stage drivers would stop to "water" the teams that pulled the coaches. My father told me that in 1941. When he was sixteen, there was a huge forest fire; and a bucket brigade was formed to save my grandfather's house. They hollered (yodeled) across the hills and called everyone they could get to help fight it. They saved the house and the massive oaks six feet in diameter, but the hemlocks were lost, leaving only the blackened snags still standing. The coach road, lined with the big flat rocks, was easier to see the; but back when the coaches were running, it must have been spectacularly beautiful in those woods.

On another part of the farm, uphill from the spring we used most, there were three flat rocks with some scratches on them. The scratch marks were dates. As I would walk through the woods with my father, he would point them out and say, "These are the graves of three Hessian soldiers."

"What's a Hessian?" I asked.

"Soldiers," he said, "now stop asking questions." Okay, I stopped asking questions, but I still wondered. We walked that path through the woods to Elma, where there was a railroad station, also a post pickup for the train, and to my Uncle Preacher's house. No, he was not a "preacher," and I do not know how he got that nickname. "Uncle Preacher" and Aunt Mary (my grandfather's sister) lived across from the RR station. On some days, we walked the RR tracks rather than through the woods because in the summer, the undergrowth was thick and sticky with razor-tooth, flesh-tearing saw briars. Also, on rainy days, we walked the tracks and across the trestles, which were very high up and slippery. I was taught how to "feel the tracks" to determine if a train was coming before I started across the trestle.

(Railroad)
Photo by: Carol R. Ellis

My father showed me how to put my ear on the rail to hear a vibration from miles away or just feel with my hand, but the train had to be much closer to feel it with just a hand. I was also told never to cross the trestle alone. I did do it once; however, I just went "across the trestle" and came back. I could not help myself. I just had to cross that trestle alone to see if I could do it. The crossties were so far apart they scared me more than a train would. When I was about halfway across, I looked down into a deep rocky gorge far beneath the trestle, and the one-hundred-plus-foot drop made me dizzy. I did not do it again. It did not look that far up from the rocky gorge when I was holding my father's hand, but doing it alone scared the wits out of me.

The spring near the graves of the Hessian soldiers was a place where hobos would jump off the train (near the village of Elma) and walk down to the spring to get a drink of water. There was an odd-shaped cup there from which the hobos could drink before they came up to the house to get food. That cup was part of my grandfather's World War I "mess kit," and I was told not to drink from it or I might get TB from one of the hobos, (Of course, I drank the fresh, icy spring water from its time and time again without any problem.) The area around the spring was home to all manner of snakes, skunks, lizards, and frogs, which usually ran when I approached the spring. We had a spring box where we cooled milk, butter, and "semi-jelled" Jell-O in the cold spring water coming from the ground. We spooned the "slimy" Jell-O over pound cake for dessert. I never had firm Jell-O until I went to school in 1955.

Photo of railroad trestle by Carol R. Ellis

Sometimes, after having a drink of water at the spring, the hobos would make their way up the hill to my grandparents' house. They would knock on the door, and my grandmother would give them a plate of food. There they sat on the front steps, if they were white, and eat whatever was left from breakfast or dinner (which was our noon meal). "Colored hobos" sat on the back steps. They told stories to catch us up on the news. My grandmother said they were "dirty, nasty, filthy old hobos, and they stink." My grandfather thought we should treat them well anyway. The C&O and the Southern railroads both had right-of-way across the property, and the hobos knew where they could stop for food and water.

Looking back on the territorial freedom I had to roam, and go from place to place, it is a wonder I survived. I not only survived, but I thrived in the natural freedom, the glorious beauty of the environment with all the available natural food just waiting for a child as "wild as a Billy goat" to come along and eat it. My early childhood freedom would leave a restless, closed-in, trapped feeling anytime I had to be inside school or church, a feeling which I could never escape until I was able to get back into my beloved and familiar woods.

I did not know it then, but we lived like early American pioneers; we were poor, but self-sufficient, and nothing more than a "link in the chain" of the history of this beautiful backwoods-my little piece of paradise.

The land itself had a bit of all the history of America: the Indians, the Revolutionary War, the plantation and slaves, the Civil War, the post-Depression and WWll-veteran hobos still existing in the '50s.

It would be many years, after having traveled many winding roads, before I put together greatness of what l had experienced in my preschool years on that small hardscrabble piece of ground we called a farm.

The Characters in The Book

Carol (me)

Daddy (my father)

Mom (my mother)

James and Mattie

PawPaw (my grandfather)

MawMaw (my grandmother)

Helen and Ree

I have chosen to describe the characters (my family) in this book because they each, in their own way, had a profound effect on my early childhood development. Their presence, and their influence, shaped my experiences and helped form the beliefs I hold-and continue to explore today-regarding the economically disadvantaged, the elderly, the physically disabled, the mentally challenged, and those who are discriminated against solely because of their race.

CAROL, ME

As a child, it was said that I was inquisitive, wild, willful, and completely unruly. Somebody had to catch me just so my hair could be combed or so I could be given a bath. I picked up on everything especially what was said of other people. If I was within earshot of conversations, the content stuck in my head and, in all likelihood, would be repeated at the most inappropriate of times. My parents had a friend in Rockfish, Virginia, named Wallace. Wallace was tall, and he smoked a cigar, and it was said he was a "sourpuss." He was also a relative. One time, out of many, Wallace came walking down the road from our house to my grandparents' house. When I laid eyes on him walking toward the house, I ran in and yelled at the top of my lungs, "Here comes old sourpuss Wallace!" Daddy cried to shut me up, but it was too late. Wallace heard every word.

If heard something once, that was it; it stuck in my head. If I saw something, it too stuck in my memory bank. The old folks got a bit paranoid with me around thinking if they said something, I would repeat it for sure.

There was no telling me not to do something. I would decide for myself whether to do it or not. I did not like whippings; bur if I wanted to do something, I would give it the "whipping rest." First, I would have to decide about the chances of getting caught. Next, I would have to decide whether I thought I would actually get a whipping if I was caught. Then I would have to decide if it was worth a whipping. One such occasion took place when I was in first grade.

Daddy had talked so much about the ''bootleggers'' who lived between our house and the little nearby community of Rockfish that I decided to go visit their home one day. l was on the school bus headed home, and the bus stopped to let the bootleggers' kids off. I told the bus driver that I was going to get off the bus and visit chem. He asked me if my father knew that I was getting off. I told him my parents knew all about it, and it was okay with them. He knew better, but I insisted and he let me off. One of the kids told me her father (the bootlegger) did not like strangers coming to the house, and I could be in a lot of trouble. One of the other girls stayed down by the road to tell her father that stranger was at their house. When her father got home from work, she told him I was there. He stayed down on the main road to wait for my father to pass by on his way home, and he flagged Daddy down and told him I was there.

In the meantime, the younger girl, who was my age, and I walked the long road up the mountainside toward the house. The house was dilapidated, and as one side fell in, the family moved to the remaining side. The house was weathered and had no paint. The mother was cooking a pot of brown beans, and she was scared to death that I was there. She asked my friend what she thought she was doing to bring me there. She said, "Your daddy is gonna' kill you both." She told her mother that it was my fault; I just got off the bus and came home with her.

The next thing I heard was a very loud "bellowing" from the woods down the hill. It was my father. He was calling me, and he did not sound happy. I looked out, and when I saw him, I knew I was in big trouble. I walked down the rickety steps and tried to talk to Daddy, but all he said was "Start walking and get in that truck." I kept trying to talk to him, but he would not talk. I got in the truck and tried to talk to him, and still, he would not talk. When we got home, I got out of the truck and ran into the house.

My mother did not know where I had been since I did not come home on the bus, and she was angry with me. She asked Daddy why I had come home with him. He told her what I had done and said he was going to give me a whipping I would never forget. He yanked his belt off so fast it whistled and snapped, and he did give me a whipping I would never forget. My grandmother heard me screaming down at her house, and she later asked my father what the racket was. She told him he should not have beaten me like that, but he was unfazed. He told her I was just too "damned hardheaded," I think if I had to do if over again, I would do the same thing. I was fascinated with the way other people lived especially when they were talked about in such colorful and interesting ways. I heard so may tales about people going into places in the hills from which they never cam back, that I wanted to see for myself. I was not particularly afraid even when I was constantly warned.

DADDY, MY FATHER

Daddy was a farm boy born in western Kentucky in a coal-mining town and moved to Nelson County, Virginia, as an infant. He struggled with poverty, rotten luck, and hard times. He was strapping, good looking, and six feet tall and was a GI in Germany in WWII where he received a Purple Heart for being wounded in combat. He was also a sharpshooter, but he learned to shoot before he was in the military. He, of necessity, learned to hunt when he was quite young. He was much beloved and little understood.

Daddy was born into a life of hardship. To characterize my father's life as one formed by poverty alone would be simplistic; it was more complicated than that. His father, PawPaw was a Bible-thumping religious fundamentalist, and "Old Testament Christian "who dominated my father with scripture and a stick. He worked and worked hard, but there seemed no end to it. The only way he could escape was to die. I was with him up until shortly before he died of lung cancer in 1987, and even then, I do not think he ever found any peace. I prayed for his soul to come around again in a more peaceful iteration.

Daddy did five things that I remember vividly. Once, a poisonous snake crawled up his leg, and he could not get it off using his hands. He told my brother to run get his gun, a .22 rifle-which was always loaded, behind the kitchen door. My brother got the gun, and Daddy shot the head off the snake while it was on his leg. I wanted to get the gun, but my father would not allow it. He never taught me to shoot because he said that since I was a girl, I did not need to learn to shoot. I did not know why I could not get the gun. To touch the loaded gun was something even I would not do; there was an ironclad rule not to touch any of the guns-usually loaded-at any time, for any reason unless told to do so. I was older than my brother, bur Daddy had taught him to handle a gun since he was about two years old.

The second thing I remember is the incident when Daddy tried to ride a milk cow. I am not sure what got into him, maybe it was Jim Beam. Anyway, he decided he would ride the cow. The cow had horns, big horns, big enough to "put a hurtin'" on anybody trying to ride her. I had a lot more respect for "dumb" cows after that. She threw him, and finally, he hit the ground with an awful thud, right in the middle of a cow pile. He got up laughing, and then he went down to the creek and "washed up."

The third thing I remember was when it was hog-killing time, and Daddy decided he would cut the pig's throat instead of shooting it between the eyes and then cutting its throat to bleed it clean. PawPaw told him not to do it because hogs are very dangerous, but Daddy decided he was going to do it his way, and that was that. By the time the hog got done with Daddy, he was a muddy, bloody mess. The pig was dead, but what a spectacle Daddy had made of himself. I am sure that if he had just shot the hog in the first place and then cut its throat with a knife, the hog would have bled out cleaner. My grandfather, who thought Daddy had ruined the hog, was not pleased with Daddy's performance that day.

The fourth thing Daddy did, which I could never forget, is put me-without a saddle-on the back of the old Belgian workhorse. He put my brother on behind me, told me to hold on right to the horse's mane, and told my brother to hold on to me. The horse's hair dug into my bare thighs like needles. Then he yelled, "Hold on," and slapped the horse on the rump which made the horse run. Off we went, down the hill behind the barn, on the back of that huge horse, holding on to that mane for dear life. He whistled one of his "country-boy whistles," and the horse turned around and came back to him. I do not know how old I was when the incident happened, but it was before I went to school and after my brother was old enough to sit on the horse. I was probably five, and he would have been about four years old.

There used to be wild-bee hives full of honey in the woods surrounding our house. Daddy was accustomed to using a ladder to get high enough and then climbing the tree with a smoking rag wrapped around a stick to thrust into the hive and drive the bees our so he could get a bucketful of honey in big hunks of honeycomb. On one occasion, he climbed the tree with the smoking rag stick, and the bucket, to plunder the beehive. The bees did not appreciate the intrusion and swarmed him. He was stuck up the tree being attacked without a free hand to fight back. He dropped the bucket and fought the bees with the smoking rag stick. There he was, up the tree, trying to protect himself from being stung and trying to stay long enough to get the honey. I thought it was funny, and I laughed, but there was nothing funny about it to him. He took on some weird positions trying to stay alive in that tree. Eventually, he got the better of the hive and, at least temporarily, ran the bees off long enough to retrieve the bucket and raid the honey. He got almost a bucket full of honey and honeycomb. He brought it in to my mother and told her not to expect any more honey-ever. She squeezed the honey out of the comb by hand and gave us the waxy comb to chew. That was the last time I tasted wild honey because Daddy kept his word.

MOM, MY MOTHER

My mother was a German war bride who met my father in Berlin during WWII. She had a good command of the English language with no hint of an accent when she came to America in 1947. As a young German girl in Berlin in WWII, she suffered abuse from her alcoholic father, experienced starvation, and had to take care of her disabled mother. My mother's two younger brothers were conscripted into the Hitler Youth, and none of the family ever saw them again. They were believed to have died on the Russian front; but once the boys-aged twelve and fourteen-were forcibly taken away, they were never heard from, or about, again. She often said that it would have taken only one bullet to kill Hitler, and she wondered why no one ever shot him. When she was six years old, Hitler came to her school, and she was one of the kids who shook hands with him. Mom was five feet ten inches tall and an athlete. She trained as an Olympic triathlete but because of WWII she never got to compete. Participating in an Olympic competition was her dream and one she never realized. She continued to swim even though she had her first heart attack many years later while swimming.

My mother's concept of America in 1947 was based on her perception of all of America as New York City, but when she arrived, the reality was altogether different. She ended up in Nelson County, Virginia, which she later described as "poorer than Appalachian poor." There was no electricity, no plumbing, and therefore no indoor bathroom, no central heat, no running water, no car for transportation, "no nothing." She often said, even coming from bombed-out Berlin, that she had gone back in time to some primitive era. She had gone back in time. The house that would become her home was built from timber cut on out land and constructed by my father and grandfather. It was a tar paper shack in which they would "camp out," with no windows installed until cold weather set in November 1949. It was there, in September of 1949, that I was brought home as an infant, the first of her five children.

My mother would later tell everyone when she introduced us as her children that I was not like her "other children." That was a true statement. For one thing I could "see" things before they happened. The other children in our family never had the territorial, or personal, freedom that I experienced. I was the firstborn with a brother following a year later and a sister born on my third birthday. As soon as I could walk, I went anywhere I wanted to and had little supervision until I was six years old.

I do not believe my mother was bigoted. She was a lifelong Republican (after coming to America) and did not like Democrats, but I do not recall her saying "nigger." Maybe she did say it, but I do not remember hearing her do so. She was also the one responsible for the end of my carefree life when she forced me to go to school.

In 1955, I was six years old and, inevitably, had to go to school. My life as I knew it had suddenly ended and from chat rime on I was a reluctant participant in any of my further education. If you have ever seen a feral cat caught up in a burlap sack, that was me-in first grade. It was not a good fit. I could not comprehend the sense of being forced to sit in a chair every day in school after riding the school bus for an hour. That was not my idea of what life should be at all. I hated school, the bus, and the other kids who just seemed to get in my way. Sometimes I would hide, and the bus would come and go, and I would tell my mother the bus never came. We had no phone, so she could not check to see if I was lying; but the next Sunday, she would see the bus driver at church and ask if he failed to come for some reason. I would have forgotten the incident, but my mother had not. I would get a whipping for lying, but it was worth it. I hated the long ride to school, and I intensely disliked most of the kids I met there because I was not used to being around other children of my age. My father had said their parents were "just a bunch of hillbilly bootleggers." (I did not know what a bootlegger was and I certainly did not know they provided the clear stuff kept in a Mason jar on a high shelf.) Besides, I never had to put up with any other kids except my brother and sister, and they did nor count because they were too little to be a bother. The good thing about those two was that they kept my mother occupied, and that left me relatively free until first grade.

After being taught to read the King James Version of the Bible around the table two times a day, especially the Old Testament, reading about Dick and Jane was just downright stupid and boring, and the story of Spot the Dog, well, that was really stupid. When asked to read out loud in school, I did it, and once was enough. I wanted to do something else. Watching and listening to other kids trying to learn to read was more than I could tolerate. They were slow and hesitant and really got on my nerves. Sometimes, I would get up of my seat and go read it for them. The teacher did not appreciate my help and often had to tell me to sir down and stay in my seat. Shortly after I went to school, my mother began working at Sears on Main Street in Charlottesville, and that is when Mattie came into our lives.

JAMES AND MATTIE

James and Mattie were a married couple with children of their own and were good friends of my parents. They were "colored" people and lived in one of the "colored" sections of Nelson County. They were well-known for being some of the finest and kindest people around, black or white. James and Daddy worked together as carpenters in Charlottesville and commuted from Nelson County, about thirty-five miles, every day together. They would ride in Daddy's truck co the Hickory Hill intersection of Route 29 and gather with others to go into town to work. Relatively speaking, gas was cheap in 1955, but carpenter labor wages were low too. Often, there was no work at all. Everybody was poor, black and white alike, and we all had at least that much in common. It used to be said that Nelson County was so poor in chose days that the crows had to pack a lunch just to fly over it.

Mattie stayed at our house while James, and my mother and father, worked in Charlottesville, and she "looked after us" She made sure I got on the bus, and she took care of my brother and sister, still at home. Mattie was no-nonsense, and we were told to obey her in no uncertain terms. The message to us was if Mattie had to give us a whipping, we would get another one when Mom and Dad got home. She was so good to us, but strict, and we knew to mind her.

One day, Mattie told my brother to stop doing something, and he said, "I don't have to do anything you say. You're just an ole nigger."

Mattie looked at him and said, "Where did you learn to talk like that?" My idiot brother said, "None of your business, you're just a nigger."

Lord, have mercy on my soul; she yanked him up and gave him a heck of a whipping. When Daddy got home. Mattie wasted no time in telling him what my little brother had said. He yanked my little brother up by the arm, with his feet off the floor, and whacked him with a belt with the other hand.

For each lick of the belt, Daddy said, "Boy-don't-you-ever-call-Mattie-a-nigger, do-you-hear-me-boy?

My idiot brother, instead of shutting up, said, "But that's what you call Mattie. You call her a nigger."

My father was defenseless and made an awkward apology to Mattie, but I do not think he was ever contrite enough to make up for himself. He knew he was bigoted; James and Mattie knew it, but to me it was the strangest thing for Daddy to call them, and other blacks, "niggers" and then give us a whipping in front of them for calling them the same thing.

PAWPAW, MY GRANDFATHER

My grandfather, PawPaw, was born in 1893 and served in WWI where he drove a twenty-mule-team munitions wagon in France. He received a commendation for his skill particularly "cornering" mule teams in France during the war. He was shot in his arm and nearly lost it and his life from the severe wounds. He received a Purple Heart for being wounded in action. He was also a sharpshooter, but he was commended for his ability to handle the mule teams. It was probably his experience with that mule team that prepared him for my entrance on the scene in 1949.

PawPaw could make many things with his pocketknife, which he kept sharp with a grinding wheel out by the smokehouse. He could dig a splinter out of his hand with it and, the next minute, peel an apple or whittle a toy for me. The stone wheel was huge to me when he allowed me to "help" him by turning it as he sharpened his tools. He kept his money in a sock in the top bureau drawer along with his twist of Red Man chewing tobacco. He was of pure Scottish descent, slightly built and bent over, quiet, frugal, and uncomplaining about his rheumatoid arthritis; and he was enormously patient with me. He was well known throughout Nelson country for his honest dealings.

My grandfather lived by the King James Version of the Bible, mostly the Old Testament, and he seemed to have a fixation with the book of Ezekiel. He quoted scripture when he worked. He quoted scripture when he milked, planted corn, and plowed; and he prayed a lot. When we were required to read the Bible twice a day, I asked questions about things I did not understand. For instance, "begat"-what is "begat"? He told me not to question the Bible because that was blasphemy. I told him I could not keep reading something I did not understand. I still got no answer.

Photo of the old smokehouse by Carol R. Ellis

We came to find our much later, PawPaw had gotten a woman pregnant, and when he learned the predicament, he married and divorced her the same day. Much later in life, when I was told about it, I said, "Well, he begat, begot, and begone." Thar is why he never told me what "begat" was.

Next to the Bible and hard work, PawPaw loved his banjo. He bought his first one from Montgomery Ward in 1917 and taught himself to play. PawPaw played his banjo on the front porch, "of an evenin'," and sang.

Both my mother and grandmother considered his music caterwauling. I loved his "pickin' and singin'," and I begged him to play every chance I got. Finally, his rheumatoid arthritis got the better of him, and he had to quit his clawhammer-style banjo pickin'.

MAWMAW, MY GRANDMOTHER

MawMaw, my grandmother, was born in Kentucky in a coal-mining country; she grew up in a mining company shack with a dirt floor. She met my grandfather when he came out to work as a coal miner with my Uncle Preacher. Uncle Preacher worked in the coalmines and brought my grandfather with him on a trip back co Kentucky. Uncle Preacher was married to PawPaw's sister Mary. Mary was a twin, but her infant sister died of scarlet fever in the are 1890s.

MawMaw was very quiet, just didn't talk much, except under her breath when PawPaw came around. If he came into the house and said anything, she would go "humph," with a kind of grunt. I asked her why she did not talk to PawPaw but never got an answer. Maybe it was that he had bccn marricd before and had a child or maybe it was because she hated the farm and the constant work grind or maybe she missed her family in Kentucky; I never knew. I told her once she and PawPaw were like "two old snappin' turtles."

She worked hard and constantly. While PawPaw did the milking at 4:00 a.m., she would start the wood fire by throwing some kerosene in the stove, jumping back, and throwing a match at it. The fire would roar up out of the woodstove in a column of fire, and she would place the place over the hole and begin breakfast. My father would repeatedly warn her she could burn the house down starring the fire with kerosene; but she just looked at him with a blank stare and threw the match. Breakfast was a big meal and consisted of biscuits, which she made in an old crockery bowl by just throwing in the ingredients-lard, flour, buttermilk, salt, soda, and baking powder-all without measuring. We had fresh eggs. fresh milk, and sausage, which had been canned in the winter. She poured the canned sausage out of the half-gallon mason jar, far and all, into and iron skillet to hear. Sometimes, in the summer, when all of the garden produce had been canned and there was the least little free time. we had to sew "sausage socks" made of the good parts of worn-our sheets and pillowcases in which to stuff the sausage. The sleeve or sock, of sausage was hung in the cellar under the house to be kept cool so it would not spoil. The outside of the sleeve may have grown moldy, but the inside was fine, and we ate it.

After breakfast, most days, MawMaw made yeast rolls and set them by the stove to rise. If I was around, she set me down to churn and make butter. I tried to hightail it out of there before she did that because sitting still for long enough to make butter was sheer torture. She put me to work for two reasons: one, so I would not run in the house and make the rolls fall and two, to keep me occupied so I would not bother her with her work. After all, in addition to everything else she had to do, she had to prepare three meals a day. If I still hung around after churning, she would send me down to the spring to put the buttermilk and butter in the spring box to chill. The spring box was inside of the springhouse, which was built directly over the spring to keep debris out of the water. A fence with a gate was built around the springhouse to keep animals out. It was said that the spring had never run dry. The water was very pure, clean, and icy cold.

In addition to making bread and churning every day, MawMaw always had beans to shell, corn to shuck, apples and peaches to can in season, and chickens to kill. When she caught and killed the chicken by wringing its neck, or having PawPaw chop its head off, she would scald it in hot water and pick the feathers off. A scalded chicken stinks. After all the outside preparation had been done, including gutting the thing, she would take it in the kitchen and cut it up. I always thought that wringing a chicken's neck was better because there was no messy blood involved the way it is when the head is chopped off and the chicken keeps flopping around the yard, spewing blood everywhere. Sometimes there would be unlaid eggs in the chicken, and we would cook and eat them right along with the meat. We ate chicken, pork, squirrel, rabbit, and venison. We almost never had beef because we did not raise beef cattle, only milk cows. MawMaw had rheumatoid arthritis and osteoporosis, with a big hump on her back, but she never complained. She also had asthma, which acted up from time to time, but I do not recall that it ever stopped her from working.

My grandmother, only five feet tall, had to do hard way. My grandfather hauled water up from the spring on the flatbed wagon pulled by the team of horses. The water was then lifted off the wagon and placed over a hot fire that had been built near the clothesline area. Once the water was hot, the laundry was put in the tub and either poked and stirred with a stick or scrubbed on a scrub board. After washing, the laundry had to be rinsed in the other tub of water. Once it was rinsed, the laundry had to be hand-wrung by bare hands to get the water out. Bigger items had to be wrung by two people twisting in opposite directions until it was completely wrung out of water. After the wringing, the clothes and bed linens were hung on the clothesline to dry. If the laundry was very heavy, like quilts, the line poles were used to prop up the line to keep the clothes off the ground. God help the kid, usually me, running in and out of the sheets for fun. That would bring out the broom for a chase and a swat when they were caught.

HELEN AND REE

Helen was Daddy's sister and the middle child. She was said to have been born breach after a three- day labor ordeal and suffered apparent oxygen deprivation. She also had childhood diabetes, but I heard everyone refer to it as "she has sugar." Helen was heavyset, and no wonder. My grandmother put sugar on everything, even in green peas, fresh from the garden. Helen loved her sweets and my grandmother made lots of pies and cakes because my grandfather loved them too. Even though he liked his sweets, he was rail thin.

As a child, I thought Helen was beautiful. From old family photographs, she like MawMaw's mother from Kentucky. She had coal black hair and deep violet blue eyes. Helen had a sweet and kind disposition, and when others in the family were against me for asking so many questions, she was my refuge. I could curl up in her lap, she would hold me, and we would take naps together on the glider swing on the front porch.

Helen could read the Bible, like the rest of us, but she could also read Reader's Digest and other magazines. She had a profound stutter when she spoke, and she had a lot of difficulty when she tried to communicate. She may have been the one most responsible for my learning to read, other than from the Bible, even before I went to school. We spent a lot of time together reading, and it benefited both of us.

REE

Marie, called Ree, was die youngest child born to my grandparents. She too was, reportedly, born breach and suffered apparent oxygen deprivation at birth. Ree had violent fits, and she was never "quite right." For one thing, she did not look like anyone else we knew of in the family. She was nearly six feet tall and big. Her eyes were crossed, they seemed to bulge out, and her hair was very thin and scraggly. She had a distinct speech impairment that made her difficult to understand, but she had a remarkable memory. She could recall any numbers that she heard and knew of all the birthdays of everybody in the family, even of long-dead relatives. She had a number fixation, and when asked about a particular Bible verse, she could not only recite the verse but quote the book and chapter.

Ree had chores, and she too, worked in the house. Mainly she swept everything in sight. She swept the floors, the stairs, the porches, and even the yard until there were bare parches with no grass. When she swept, the dirt made a huge cloud of red dust settled back on the porch she had just swept.

When the black workers were on the farm, they avoided her. They did not know what to make of her, and she could be a scary sight when she had one of her fits. I never knew if she liked us kids or hated us or perhaps did not think of us at all.

Note:

For most of Helen's and Ree's lives, they were largely ignored. They did not seem to count for much, except maybe to my grandmother. She loved them just as they were. I never knew how my grandfather felt about them except he was very protective of them both and said they were perfect the way God had made them. They were both special to me. They were a part of the family constellation and had a very real presence in life on the farm. They had personalities, and though profoundly handicapped from a disadvantaged birth, they managed to make a big contribution coward the extraordinary workload. I still have the quilts they made. Without Helen and Ree, my life would not have been the same; my earliest learning experiences would not be so vivid, colorful, and permanent.

THE CHILDHOOD STORIES REGARDING RACISM

MY FIRST HOG KILLING

One of the main functions of a farm is to provide and preserve enough food for the family to last through all seasons. If we were going to eat it, we had to catch it, kill it, grow it, and preserve it. If we had enough, we traded goods for something we did not have, like flour, sugar, or salt. One of the biggest farm events of the year was hog-killing time. The perfect killing time was dictated by the weather. It had to be cold with no chance of warm weather returning because if it did get hot again, the meat would spoil. Hog-killing time was always after Thanksgiving.

My first memory of hog-killing rime was a dreary, bone-chilling cold December day in 1952. The air was icy with snow flurries, and my breath seemed to freeze my lungs. Still, I would not have been inside anyway; and though I was told not to go out in the cold, I had to see, and be part of, what was going on. There was nobody there who could police what I was up to anyway; every available body was busy with the hog killing.

I was three years old, and I know I was three because my baby sister had just been born on my birthday in September; and my brother, born between the two of us, was too little to come outside by himself.

It was barely daylight when I ran headlong down the steps off the back porch, through the chickens, and looked toward the smokehouse. What a sight! About the same time, I took my first frozen gasp; a penetrating.

unforgettable, suffocating stench mugged my nose. I put my bare hand over my nose and mouth, trying to keep the smell out as I watched two big barrels over an open fire steaming in the cold morning air. Then it happened. l was engulfed in the horrible sight.

Illustration by Carol R. Ellis

Two black men were holding a rod with a huge dead hog on it, lashed at the hind feet and hanging head down, and they had put the whole pig in the barrel of hot water. As they lifted the pig out, it stunk. It was awful and stifling and made me hold my breath rather than breathe. It was like nothing I had ever smelled. After they scalded the hog, they hung it up between the forks of two trees. The hog's head was off to the side in a big dish pan. So, there it was-hanging, steaming, and stinking to high heaven, and the men were scraping the hair off. Then they cut that pig from stem to stern and gutted it. The steaming guts rolled out into a tub, and the black people got the "chitlins." I wanted to throw up, but I was rivered by the sight. I am not sure why I never associated that stinking mess with the delicious meals my grandmother cooked. I suppose if I had, I would just have starved. Then again, when it was time to eat, everybody was so hungry; nobody had time to think about how the food got to the table.

Trying to get anyone's attention to ask anything was out of the question. The hogs occupied everybody's time but mine. I wanted to know what they were going to do next, and I was told to stop asking so many questions or I would have to go back to the house. I decided to go back to the house anyway because my grandmother was stirring a big pot over the roaring hot woodstove. I asked her what she was doing, and she told me she was making lard and cracklin's. "What are cracklin's?" I asked. My grandmother said, "I don't have time to fool with you, and if you don't stop asking so many questions, you are going to have to go back outside." It turns out she was rendering lard. The cracklings were the little crispy bits of fat that did nor render, and she put them in a bucket behind the stove. I had no notion whatsoever of how dangerous "rendering lard" on a woodstove could be. It was a very real fire hazard and had to be accomplished with extrcmc caution. The liquid far could nor splash out onto the stove or the whole house could burn. It was a touchy operation.

"Can you eat cracklin's?" I asked.

"Yes, Carol, you can eat them, but if you do, you'll be sick as a dog. Now don't get in that bucket of cracklin's. We'll have some cracklin' bread later, and besides, we've got enough to do without you gettin' sick on us." Cracklin' bread is corn bread made with the crispy fat cracklings added before it is baked. I grabbed a big handful of cracklins' and then I went back outside to see if I was needed anywhere there.

By the time I got back out to the slaughtering area, there was another pig hanging from the tree, and the first one was in big pieces. The men had put some boards across the handcrafted sawhorses to make a cutting table. I think that was the first rime I really noticed the black men in the curious way children take things in. They were, it seemed, really big and tall. My grandfather and my father were the only white men there; and there were, as best I can remember, four or five black men; and they were lifting, cutting, and hauling pieces to the smokehouse and salting the meat down in the saltbox. They also hauled the washtubs of fat tso the back porch where my grandmother could get it, take it to the kitchen, and render the lard. They also separated out the parts on hog's head, like the ears, jowls, snout, tongue and the brains, which my grandfather loved with eggs. Everything but the brain in a hog's head went into souse meat. It is ground up, congealed and fried for breakfast.

The blacks were not allowed in the house; they could only put the tubs on the porch. I asked why the men could not come into the house, and I was told, "Because they're niggers, that's why." I saw the black guys a smile a wary smile at one another but they said nothing. That would not be the last time one of my questions yielded one of those looks from black men.

JIGABOOS AND PICKANINNIES

All of my preschool years were spent on the farm with me extended family, consisting of my great-grandparents, my grandparents, my great-aunts and uncles, my aunts, and my mother, father, brother, and sisters. My life was formed by me influences of not only the human contact but the wild out- of-doors where I spent all my time. If I was not feeding the chickens, bringing in firewood, hanging up clothes, or hauling water in buckets up the hill from the spring, I was climbing trees or eating cherries, apples, plums, peaches, fox grapes, chinquapins, or whatever was in season. I was in constant motion, skipping from place to place. My great-grandparents lived across Dutch Creek, and there was an open ford in the stream where we crossed with the horse and wagon and, rarely, with a car. When the creek was down, we walked through the water to cross. When the creek was up because of a big rain, we walked a slippery, mossy foot log across the creek to get there. The water was deep and rolling yellow. I was told repeatedly never to go into the creek alone but I did anyway. Dutch Creek ran parallel to me train cracks where the blacks and hobos used to get to the spring on the farm.

There were times when there was more work than the family could handle, and we hired the black (colored) folk who brought their children with them. Hog-killing time was not the only time the "coloreds" came to the farm. When it was hay-cutting time, they came to work. When the combine was rented, and hauled to the farm, they came.

When a building had to be built, repaired, painted or roofed, they came. When the colored needed work done on their buildings, my grandfather did not hesitate help them with their work in mum of the work was accomplished through the barter system. The workers, black or white, did not want kids in the way because of the extreme danger and the distraction.

It was then we were told, "Go over there and play with the jigaboo and pickanninnies and stay out of the way.

I asked my father, "Why do you call them jigaboos and pickanninnies?"

He said, "Can't you just do what you are told and stop asking so many questions?"

I told him, "If you answer my questions, I'll stop asking. I just want to know if I am a jigaboo or pickaninny."

He said, "For cryin' out loud, Carol, will you stop asking questions all the time? No, you are nor a jigaboo or a pickaninny because you are white."

I did not feel like they were any different from me; they were just a different color with different hair. They had names. They had families. They were people too. When they ran, fell down, and cut themselves, their blood was red like mine; and I just did not get it. The only difference I could see was that they looked different. I thought they were beautiful. In fact, when it rained and I could find a good mud puddle, I rubbed the mud all over me so I would look like chem. All that effort ever yielded was a bucket of cold water dumped over my head and a hard scrubbing to gee the mud off.

Since my father seemed upset enough to give me a whipping for asking "too many questions," I decided to ask my grandfather, who never gave me a whipping, why the colored kids were called "jigaboos and pickanninnies." One morning, we were walking to the barn to do the milking. I had one of the empty milk buckets, and he had the other bucket and the coal oil lantern to light the path. It was 4:30 a.m. and black-dark with the sky full of sparkling stars and a chill in the air.

Photo of original chestnut barn by Carol R. Ellis

"PawPaw," I said, "why does Daddy call the colored kids jigaboos and pickanninnies?"

He said, "Why do you ask?" "Because I want to know," I said. "Well," he said, "that's not a nice name." "So why does he call them that?"

"I don't know," he said.

"Do you call chem jigaboos and pickanninnies?"

"No," he said.

"So why does Daddy call them that?"

He said, "You'll have to ask him." I could not get answers out of anybody.

I was beginning to think adults did not know much of anything.

By then, we were at the barn, and it was time to milk the cows. I never did get an answer. Paw Paw sat on the little three-legged milking stool he had made and milked the cow while she chewed and swished her tail. He taught me how to milk but almost never let me do the milking because he just wanted to get it done, and he was good at it and faster than I was. We carried the steaming, foamy milk back to the house where my grandmother had breakfast ready. I liked to drink the still-warm milk for breakfast, and the cream would already be rising to the top. It was still dark: there was coal oil lamp in the middle

My father replied, "No, James is not a nigger. He is our friend. Why would you ask such a question?"

I replied, "Well, you said Whistlin' Sam couldn't ride on the front seat because he was a nigger, and James is brown like Whistlin' Sam, so is James a nigger?"

Now James knew Whistlin' Sam as well as my father did, and a slow grin came across James's face. He did not say another word, and neither did I, but I never forgot it. In fact, I have thought of it often. Mattie had challenged my brother about his use of the "nigger" word, and I wonder why James did not say something about it to my father. Maybe it was because there was a special "knowing" between James and Daddy. James was like the brother Daddy never had, and I knew they had a deep friendship.

SEARS ON MAIN STREET

In the 1950s Sears Roebuck was located on West Main Street in Charlottesville, Virginia. Most Friday nights, we would go into Charlottesville to do grocery shopping and look around Sears just to get acquainted with "city life." My mother would do the grocery shopping while Daddy sat in the car, smoking his corncob pipe or an unfiltered Camel cigarette. We kid could go with Mom to the grocery store as long as we behaved and did not ask for anything, or we could go next door to Sears to look around. We got the standard lecture, "Don't run in the store, don't touch anything, and don't get into trouble."

On one particular trip, it was hot as Hades, and none of us wanted to sit in the car with Daddy and who he was mostly did not just want us wanted around anyway. He had worked hard all day, and he was tired and just wanted a little "peace and quiet." So, my brother and I went into Sears where it was air-conditioned; and they had a candy department with every kind of fudge, hard candy-loose and by the piece-if you had any money, which we did not. Mostly, we just looked and drooled until we were told to buy something or get lose. Anyway, there was something I had wanted to do in Sears for a long time, and this seemed to be as good a rime as any.

I told my brother we should go to the bathroom at the back of the store. He was more than willing; it was something to do. Now in those days, the Sears store had segregated bathrooms and drinking fountains.

There was a big sign over the bathroom for colored folks and another over the other bathroom for white folks. I told my brother to go into the colored men's room and see what it looked like, and I would go to the colored women's room. I don't know if my brother thought something would eat him if he went into the "colored restroom" or if our father's words telling us not to go in there or we'd get a whipping bothered him, but he was reluctant.

He said, "You know Daddy told us not to go in there."

"I know what he said, but he's not here, and we can be quick, now go."

I had convinced him to go, and watched to make sure he did, and then I ran into the colored women's restroom. I did not see anything particularly strange, so I came back out. It looked just like the white women's bathroom. My brother was already standing outside the restroom area, and we both looked at the water fountains. One was marked colored, and the other was marked white. We decided to try the drinking fountain too. They both tasted equally bad. It was city water, not the spring water we were used to.

About that time, we saw Mom and Dad walking down the middle aisle toward the back of the store, and they did not look too happy.

"Where have you two been?" they asked.

"Little brother had to go to the bathroom," I said.

"No, I didn't, you wanted to look at the nigger bathrooms," he said.

I stiffened up and got ready for another near-death experience.

"Didn't I tell you not to go in there? Didn't I tell you to stay out of that place?"

I just nodded my head and looked down.

"Then why did you do if anyway?" he asked.

"I just had to see if it was different, that's why, and it's nor. It's just like the white one," I said defensively.

My brother just had to pipe in, saying, "Yeah, and the water tastes the same too."

I think my little brother was trying to get me killed, and he may not have realized it, but his life was in jeopardy too.

"What do you think we should do with these two?" Daddy asked my mother. Then they laughed.

"Come on and get in the car so we can go home, and the next time I tell you not to do something, I expect you to listen."

If he only knew!

HELEN'S FUNERAL

As mentioned previously, my father had two sisters. Both had childhood diabetes. They never went to school because they could not get to the one-room school at Elma and because my grandfather did not want them exposed to people who would make fun of them. Since I had been told J could not ask PawPaw about them, I did not know if he felt a sense of shame for them or himself. So, they stayed home and, to the extent they were able, worked in the house, cleaning up or sewing together quilt squares from worn- out clothing, curtains, or feed sacks. My grandmother did not want to, or could not, take the time to teach them to cook; so, they never learned. Nobody thought they should be anywhere near fire. She did reach them to feed the chickens, shuck corn, snap beans, churn, haul water from the spring, and get in firewood mostly because she needed the help.

Helen was the sweet one, and I liked to help her with her chores. She had a stutter when she talked or tried to read the Bible. Along with me, Helen and Ree had to learn to read the Bible, and they did. Ree, as we called Marie, was crazy wild. She would have what we called fits. You never knew when she would jump up and flail her arms wildly and throw something. My mother told me that one time, Ree pushed her, while she was pregnant with me, into the woodstove; and my dad flung

Ree across the room and told her if she ever did that again, he'd kill her. Daddy despised her, and she was afraid of him; and other than my grandfather, he was the only one who could come close co controlling her. She was strong too. One time, I was out on the back porch; she was doing the wash in a large washtub with a scrub board, and she picked up the entire huge tub full of water, scrub board, and all and threw it on me. It scared me half to death, but I was afraid to tell Daddy for fear he really would kill her. l went into the kitchen and told my grandmother, and she told me to just leave her alone and not go near her.

On occasion, when I slept on a pallet made of quilts on the floor beside my grandparents' bed, Rec would come downstairs and appear in the doorway and whisper, "I'm gonna kill you." Then as quietly as she appeared, she would disappear; go back to her room; close the door; and make hideous, loud animal sounds for what seemed like the rest of the night. I could also hear her throwing furniture though she did not have but a few pieces in her room.

After a while, Helen began to slow down, and she seemed to just kind of waste away. When she started to lose weight, she was in bed a lot. She was put in the "front room" next to the kitchen in the two-over-two farmhouses. People started to come visit her, stand by the bed, and pray. We, as kids, were told to be quiet and not to run, jump, or act wild in the house. Of course, I asked why, and I was told that Helen was sick. Nobody ever said she was dying from kidney failure due to diabetes. I found that out later.

When Helen died, there was a service in a small church in Elma, and people came from miles around. We were all in the church for the service, and I heard glorious singing. I thought it was angels-I honest to God did. When we filed out of the church to go to the adjoining cemetery, I saw a group of black people standing to the left of the steps, and they were singing, "Swing Low, Sweet Chariot." They nodded their heads to us as we came out of the church.

I asked why they were not in the church singing because no one in the church was singing. My father said, "Because they are niggers, and they have their own church."

To this day, I still do not understand why those beauciful people had to stand outside the church and sing. It still makes me cry co remember that occasion. They had come out of respect, and they had to stand outside.

Photo of Old Church at Elma by Carol R. Ellis

ABOUT VINEGAR HILL

Vinegar Hill in the 1950s, and before, was the "colored section" of Charlottesville, Virginia. No one seems to know exactly why it was named Vinegar Hill. It was also called Niggertown or Shantytown. le was a thriving community with black-owned mom-and-pop grocery stores, funeral homes, a beautiful church, beauty salons, and the notorious Blue Moon Diner. It was a little town within a small town. Mostly, the colored folk who called Vinegar Hill home stayed within the confines of their own community and seemed to have had little need, or desire: to venture out to other areas of the town. When they did venture out, it was noticed.

In the I 960s, a Joe of Vinegar Hill was razed by developers, and office buildings were put up. Some historic buildings were lost because of new development. The size of the space allowed the black community began to shrink, and it was being squeezed out not only by commercial enterprise but by the expansion of the University of Virginia. It seemed like downtown was expanding west on Main Street, and the university was expanding east, swallowing up the vibrant and "colorful" Vinegar Hill community. The "colored section" was being systematically squeezed physically, economically and socially from both directions.

In 1968, on a hot, humid August afternoon, I was driving home after work, from downtown east on Main Street, and my car ran out of gas. It was smack in front of a score on Vinegar Hill at 5:00 p.m. on Friday, There I was, in the middle of traffic, not able to move an inch.

I looked to my right and saw four big black men walking toward my car. I froze. My heard was pounding so hard I heard it in my ears. and I thought my head was going to explode. I did not know what they were going to do, and it was then there I faced my fear of "black people." I was utterly helpless. My first thought was that they were going to rob me and beat me up because I was white. I had no money on my person, which is why the car was empty. Just as the instantaneous fear coursed through my veins, one of the men told me to put my car in neutral. I did not know what to expect, but I did it. Then the four of them pushed the car off to the side so it would not hold up traffic. The steering was very difficult because it was power steering, but I was so scared I managed it. I do not remember how I got home that day or how I got gas in the car.

After the car was safely out of the way, I got out and thanked the men for the help. I had to apologize because I had no money to give them for the wonderful help they had provided.

One of the men said, "That's all right, ma'am, we don't want no money." I felt even worse.

I told them again, "I'm sorry, I don't have any money, but I am so grateful for your help." The words rang hollow in my own ears not only because I felt so unable to repay them but because of the fear I felt when they approached me. The feeling of fear was so erroneous, so useless, and just plain wrong compared to the kindness they had shown me. It was the first time in my adult life I had to face the honest-to-God prejudice in myself that I would have sworn I did not have.

After that incident that I decided that the best way to repay those men was to rid myself of the stereotypical racial notions I still harbored. It was a very big step in my very small life.

WHEN DADDY DIED

On April I 1987, Daddy was diagnosed at the University of Virginia Hospital with terminal lung cancer. He was given a few months to live. The cancer had engulfed his esophagus and trachea, and it was inoperable. He would have to be created with radiation. When I found out about the diagnosis, I fell to the floor and cried uncontrollably for a long time. Then I picked myself up and said, "Okay, now that I have that out of the way, I need to see what has to be done to help Mom and Dad get through whatever it is they have to go through next."

In the ensuing months, I would drive to Daddy's house and bring him into Charlottesville for his radiation treatments. He had been advised not to drive at that point. That time, traveling to the hospital was the most I think I had ever had to talk with him. We did not talk much about the cancer; we talked about getting the lawn mower blades sharpened so he could mow the grass, or we talked about the weather. I wanted to know more about his childhood, his time spent in World War II in Germany, France, and Italy, but he did not want to talk about any of it. He would say, "You don't want to hear about that old stuff." That meant he did not want to talk about it, and I did not press the issue.

In 1987, there was talk of Jesse Jackson running for president. Of course, that fact was one Daddy was not happy to hear. In the summer of 1987, Daddy had to be hospitalized for a procedure to open up his trachea so he could breathe. I went to visit him while he was in the hospital and while I was there, I casually told him I was going to vote for Jesse Jackson. He got so agitated and even though he could hardly speak, he said, "Well, I just had one less daughter. No daughter of mine is going to vote for a nigger!" The other patient in the bed next to Daddy nearly choked when he laughed and said, "You are the best thing that could happen to him right now, you are good for him." I told the man I did not think had ever been the best thing that happened to Daddy. He said, "Just look how he came alive when you said what you did."

Not too long after that, my father died at 12:05 a.m. on November 15 which was my grandfather's birthday. I have often wondered if I could have ever made a difference in his thinking. I do not believe I could have, no matter how much time we had together. I stood my ground, and he stood his.

SOME THOUGHTS ON CURRENT EVENTS IN 2008

POLITICAL CORRECTNESS

Racism is about feelings of extreme dislike about people who are different, whether because of race, ability, nationality, or religion, and the subsequent discriminatory behavior practiced toward those people. Racism differs from political correctness in that the latter is sometimes used as an attempt to mask racist feelings through careful speech so as not to betray those underlying attitudes. Words can be carefully chosen so as not to appear racist, but racism can still exist on the part of the speaker. That is not to say there are not some racially charged words, which are inflammatory and should not be used publically or privately by anyone of any race. One of those words is nigger.

This issue of political correctness seems to have caused more damage than it has cleared up regarding what is, and is not, racially or otherwise, offensive. It is hard to say something in a straightforward manner without offending someone, or having what you say misunderstood by someone. Consequently, endless wasted time is spent on having to explain what was intended in the first place. That which is written, spoken, even what is placed in political cartoons in many countries, can be explosive to someone, somewhere, of some race, some political persuasion, or religion. Political correctness can be a threat to free speech and honest dialogue. How can race relations be discussed if words have to be so parsed that the issue cannot be dealt with honestly? I am not in favor of anyone deliberately insulting individuals or groups. I am also not in favor of someone, seeking our and finding, something objectionable just to claim discrimination for personal or political purposes. That is just nonsense. Sometimes, even one word has been taken out of context and exaggerated out of proportion from the original intent, and suddenly, there is a news story about it.

Real issues are sometimes obscured by the news that one political candidate allegedly said something untoward about another when the candidate speaking was just speaking and not aiming slings and arrows at the other. We all who hear know what was said in the news (ad nauseam) and we have the wits to decipher for ourselves what was intended. Then after all was said, about was said, we still may have no idea where the candidates stand on certain critical issues such as national security, health care reform, equal education, immigration, reform, social security and death penalty, social justice, a woman's right to choose, the abysmal economy, truth-in-lending, infrastructure improvement, and last but not least, that illegal and immoral war in Iraq! The brunt of that "war of misguided choice" has been disproportionately thrust upon the poor and nonwhite soldiers in what I refer to as economic discrimination, but it seems that when that issue is mentioned it is not politically correct. Far too much time is spent in the news media trying to make story out of allegedly misspoken words (especially those words deemed politically incorrect) rather than telling the truth about real news that affects all of us daily.

In today's political environment, a male African-American senator (Obama) and a white female senator (Clinton) were both running for the Office of the President of the United States of America. Obama could not even refer to himself as different without being accused of playing the race card. It is mostly the white politicians who accuse him of playing the race card. Give me a break! Speeches can be a minefield for, not only the candidates, but for their surrogates. Supporters and, even in some cases, volunteer workers are seeking special recognition by making unauthorized statements, on behalf of the campaign, that turn out to be a political blunder. Misunderstandings, based on language, happen ever day and in may places, regarding a host of issues. In the current campaign, we have heard charges of racism and sexism being hurled back and forth because of sometimes-careless speech.

Recently, I used the word "oriental" to describe someone, and I was informed, in no uncertain terms, that was "politically incorrect" and that I should have used the term "Asian." The person correcting me was from the Washington, D.C., area and well "up" on political correctness, but it seems the only way I can stay on top of it is to commit a faux pas, which is sure to be jumped on by somebody. I have been called a lot of things by a lot of individuals, but I never took offense at any of it; I just considered to the source and dismissed it. In my corporate working days, I was referred to as the bitch more than once usually because I did a superior job of whatever I was assigned to do; and that, somehow, made other people "upset." I often came in early to get special projects done just because the phones did not start ringing at 7:00 a.m. I kept in close contact with customers who had good things to say about me; but because I was a female, it was resented, and I became the brunt of the B word. (I know, I know, the B word is an insult and much more degrading than mere political incorrectness.) The point is that I was not offended (that may have been what caused some to call me the B-word). I actually had a boss who called me a "razor-tongued, rhino-hide," when I went into his office to resign. Some women would have been terribly hurt, and rightfully so because everyone has the right not to be called a degrading name. Then again, political correctness, or gender discrimination, was not the legal, or social, issue men that it has since become.

Human verbal degradation against another human being, in one form or another, has been around since there have been people, but that certainly does not make it right. Words, and how they are used, are more important than ever in 2008 as we move forward in the evolution of thought and subsequent action. Political correctness is an issue in policies. (Remember a Virginia congressman and his Macaca moment?) He dropped "plumb out of sight" after that one careless remark. I am very sure he did not realize what he had said until the political incorrectness of the reference to a reporter exploded in the news. He was a victim of his own cultural ignorance at a time when many cultures overlap in any given political gathering.

In America, speech has to be very guarded lest someone be offended by a remark made without the speaker's coral comprehension of various meanings. Innocent mistakes can be made in the usage of a word, but political correctness has become a fact of life. If not correct, it can become a veritable minefield for anyone who wishes to express an opinion in order to be a community, environmental, political, or religious activist, journalist, teacher, pastor, speaker, or even a writer. I once heard someone in a speech use the expression "old maid school teacher" to describe an individual. The speaker was confronted by a distinguished woman in the audience who had been a professor and was single. He was mortified that he may have offended her, and he did apologize profusely but never made that mistake again. Actually, he was more embarrassed than she was offended.

Then of course, there are those who make a living deliberately saying things that fly in the face of political correctness. Some radio talk show hosts, so-called shock-jocks", and political writers spew obnoxious speech on the radio and in books. There is a large audience for their negative, radical outlook comprised of venomous dialog regarding anyone who does not espouse their particular view of the word in "basic and white," which is simplistic and, in my opinion, nihilistic to extremes, I wonder if, in their "heart of hearts," when they are utterly alone with their conscience, they consider themselves to be racist or nonracist?

__What you are stands over you the while; and thunders so loudly, I cannot hear what you say to the contrary.__
-Ralph Waldo Emerson

EMBRACING DIVERSITY

Once, while I was attending a very formal dinner party given by a friend with an English title, everyone around the cable was taking turns talking about their ideal view of the world. When my turn came, I was not sure what I was going to say, but I was confident something would emerge. Then without warning, I heard myself say, "I want to be in the world when the last person realizes they are part of all the others." Well, you could have heard the proverbial pin drop. When the silence was just a bit too uncomfortable, the hostess said dismissively, "Carol, you are such an idealist." After that, things got back to the normal superficiality and skated along swimmingly with talk of world travel and how the weather was in Milan just the week before. There was also talk of how a farm in Virginia is a wonderful tax write-off, but "one really had to make a living elsewhere in order to hire the workers to maintain the farm and pay the taxes."

One person actually said chat with such a beautiful world, especially all of the long white sandy beaches, she did not think the handicapped should be allowed to go out in public and spoil the view for all of the "beautiful people." I wondered what the hell I was doing there. There was as much diversity at that function as there is in a loaf of white bread without the crust. All that seemed to be important was how they looked, what designers they were wearing, where they had been, and who they knew. Now, I will grant you, there was some power represented there, bur it seemed lackluster and somehow flat or one dimensional. The most exciting thing that happened was before dinner when I dropped my hors d'oeuvre place, along with my champagne glass, as I tried to catch my place. I stooped down to pick it up, and suddenly, there were two men, one holding each of my arms lifting me up as the hostess said, "Carol, we don't pick that up, it will be done." It was done very quickly. It never happened, the whole mess was denied; it was done so quickly the n1usicians never stopped playing. I gradually stopped attending those "functions," not because I did not like the glamour, the food, the gorgeous surroundings straight out of a fairy tale, but because there was such sameness, such perfection in everything. The grounds were perfect; the swans on the lake were perfect, even the full moon reflecting in the lake at just the right time for dancing on the veranda was perfect. At the time, I did not know why I felt so disconnected from that scene, or why amid such opulence, I felt empty. Soon I recognized that the thinking of those people was very different from my own. I would not be an instrument of change in their thinking nor could I adapt to theirs.

I enjoy getting to know people from different backgrounds, different colors and different cultures. I am fascinated by all kinds of looks, languages, foods and customs, and I want to smell it, eat it, dance the dance, and be a part of all of it. Living in a rural environment means less contact with different kinds of people, and I now miss chat aspect of city living where every day means exposure to interesting and varied aspects of humanity.

Our country is much stronger for having diversity to contribute to economic, political, social, and technical growth. It was founded on diversity, and any attempt to rein in diversity is economically limiting. Somewhere in the vastness of diverse humanity is a child, an African-American, an Asian, or a disadvantaged white child who, when properly recognized and educated, may come up with a cure for cancer, a better form of energy to power our planet with less pollution, an approach to universal peace, reach further into our galaxy, a new gene which would explain currently incurable diseases, or a way to stop the spread of viruses yet unleashed. We muse, all of us, seek to nurture intellectual curiosity and growth in children of all races, religions, and cultures.

When the global community puts as much stock in the intellect of every child as we put into other natural resource acquisitions such as oil, we will prosper economically. Intellectual capacity is a natural resource upon which the very survival of mankind will depend. When a child in Darfur, or in the United States for that matter, dies of starvation, we do not know what might have been in the life of that child that could have advanced all of mankind. Yet it seems there are only a few voices calling out in the vastness of time for someone to do something. Awareness is growing; action to make a palpable difference has been much slower.

IT WASN'T ABOUT HATRED- IT WAS ABOUT THE MISBEGOTTEN NOTION OF RACIAL INFERIORITY

The fact that my dad called people "niggers" was not so much about hatred for them as a people but rather a lack of awareness, a lack of education and understanding. My father had to leave school in the third grade when he attended school at the little one-room schoolhouse at Elma, Virginia. Since my grandfather took him out of school as a very young child because he was needed on the farm, he was not exposed to a lot of people until he was drafted into the army in World War

Some have told me they think the military in WWII is probably where he learned to be racist. After coming home from the war, my father's only dream in life was to work for the railroad and become a train engineer; but because he was still needed on the farm, and put on a guilt trip by my grandfather, he never realized that dream, nor did he ever forget it. That unrealized dream may have been the source of much of his bitterness coward the world in general.

As a child of eight years of age, and the only son, he had to work like an adult, feeding the livestock, plowing with the horse-drawn plow, chopping firewood, feeding the larger livestock like the horses and cows, and slopping hogs. He must have had a very bad experience in snowy weather because he absolutely hated snow, and no matter how many times l asked him why he hated snow, he would not tell me. As a child, there was no playtime for him, as he would later tell me his life was about work. He grew resentful, sullen, and withdrawn with his lot in life; and when he died in 1987 of lung cancer, he still harbored that resentment.

Daddy, in all my memories of him, was always a hard worker; it was all he knew. Though he worked hard, he never seemed to be able: to catch a break. I remember him coming home from work, having been laid off, and telling my mother there would be no more paychecks for the foreseeable future until things picked up. "He would take odd jobs, anything that became available just to make some money. One vivid memory was of him coming home with his hands split and bleeding because he repaired a roof in very cold, windy conditions just to get paid something. He did not have gloves, but he had rags wrapped around his hands. No one else would do the work, and I guess people knew he was desperate.

My father was not a mean man at all; and what seemed like hatred, or least incense dislike, of black people was because, for some reason, he thought they were just "plain inferior" people. In reality, the only difference between him, and them, was that they were a different color. They were poor; he was poor. They had to work hard; he had to work hard. Their houses were small and shabby, and his house was small and shabby. He, for many years, had to ride one of the workhorses to get anywhere, or walk; and so, did they if they were lucky enough to own a horse. Poverty was the great equalizer, but Daddy did not see it that way. All other things being equal, he was better off because he was white; and that made him, in his eyes, at least racially superior to them.

THE EVOLUTION IN THINKING ABOUT EQUALITY

It is now 2008, exactly forty-nine years since our family left the farm in Nelson Country in 1959. Women, including myself and African-Americans, have made some hard-won progress economically and socially. The hard-won progress has been the result of individual hard work, dogged determination, and sheer stamina in the face of the stiff winds of opposition. In spite of those gains, full social, racial, and economic justice remains out of reach for a huge segment of the population and is, in fact, slipping into reverse due to the current downturn in out economic climate. Poverty is spreading through rapid downward mobility especially among the groups that have worked so hard to make advances on the elusive slippery slope to upward class mobility.

The lack of ability to sustain our economy has been the result of corporate greed and governmental incompetence waging war on the very American citizens, and consumers, the sustain both the government and corporations. Just as the wealthy exploited the poor and ignorant whites and blacks in the Old South, corporations today continue exploiting the poor and ignorant, whether in the United States or in foreign countries. Immigration, especially from Mexico, is encouraged by our government and corporations in order to import and exploit poor workers who will settle for lower wages than would Americans. What American taxpayers get for the effort is the importation of a permanent "third world underclass" to do the hard labor and the dirty work that we are told Americans do not want to do. It is not because Americans will not do the work, but they will not do it for less than a "living wage." As I write this, the price of a gallon of gas is rapidly approaching the same amount as the minimum wage. In Charlottesville, Virginia, there is a shortage of nurses and teachers. With housing costs prohibitive, those professionals have to live in outlying counties and commute. Gas prices are prohibitive now too. Every American's health, and safety, is compromised by a lack of leadership and corrupt and incompetent management on all levels of government, local state and federal. How is the current complex situation, which can hardly be comprehended by most citizens, let alone managed, be economically sustainable and just?

Call me a cynic, if you will, but the government is passively importing poor people into this country, by looking the other way and not addressing immigration, to service the Bush "war machine." It seems to be the ultimate form of negative racial activism. Instead of dragging humans to the United States as were the African-American slaves, the gates are opened, the government eye is closed, and illegal immigrants walk into what they think is a better life. Mexican immigrants, and others, may suppose they are "sneaking" in for an economic opportunity and a better life, but actually, they are unwittingly volunteering their low-wage servitude under the boot heel of corporate power and exploitation. After they have been in the United States for a while, they will no doubt be offered an "opportunity" to serve the "war machine" by serving in our woefully understaffed military in order to qualify for citizenship -that is, if they live. The politicians know full well what would happen if they were to even suggest a draft in the United States.

Corporate wealth, in America and around the globe, continues to accumulate on the backs of the powerless, the defenseless, and the disenfranchised that have to take what is offered for their labor just to survive. We have not done away with slavery; it has been cleverly redesigned and camouflaged by exporting it to third world, less developed nations where the people will accept anything offered, however small, in return for a day's work. There is another advantage to exporting slavery; we do not have to look it in the eye everyday and acknowledge our individual responsibility for the plight. We can no longer go to sterile, orderly, well-stocked grocery stores, malls, and big-box stores and shop for the things without thinking about how those things got here and at what price to the individual producing them. The economic impact of gutting the world's human, and natural, resources is coming home to roost in the form of higher food and energy prices; the consequences are now irreversible.

Now that we have an environment in peril, unnecessary wars under way, and food shortages in much of the world, an adjustment in American thinking and our own concomitant lifestyle downsizing is necessary. The United States cannot treat its labor force, its ethnically diverse population, with reckless abandon as if those individuals were dispensable and of no consequence. They are, in fact, the collective Atlas holding up the American economy by working and paying taxes and by being consumers. Their heads are bent; their backs are crumbling under the weight of corporate greed coupled with government incompetence. We are our own worst enemy operating from position of "unenlightened self-interest" (take off on Adam Smith).

It has become a matter of national security to tap into all human talent for the country to be economically sustainable. By not doing so, the United States has developed a permanent underclass which can be sustained only by welfare, or crime, which is on the fast track to making a true third world country within out country, or worse yet, make our country a third world country. Face it, the more people who occupy a space, the less opportunity there is for each individual. With millions of people coming in to this country, the slices of the "opportunity pie" keep getting smaller and smaller with each passing year. As a result, equality is an economic mandate which may now be permanently out of reach for any of us. The common sense in this notion of equality seems to have completely eluded the Congress of the United States. It is as if once elected the prerequisite to actually serving is to check all brains outside the door before entering and with the powers that be saying, "no need to worry; we will give you a new brain better suited to thinking about your own welfare." This is the only possible way to explain the shortsighted, irrational, empty-headed, destructive policies that come out of that once-noble body. Congress can take comfort in knowing they actually accomplished something; the near total destruction of the United States of America.

The millions of jobs that have been exported to third world countries do not add to our economy. The people who are producing, in more and more cases, inferior and dangerous good to be imported into our country for consumption don't spend the small amount of money they make in our country. With the paltry wages they make, they cannot buy the increasingly fewer manufactured goods we still have to export to their countries. We have not only exported jobs that Americans could do but permanently exported the revenues those Americans would make and spend in our domestic economy and upon which they pay taxes. Current economic policy is rapidly eroding the tax base at a time when this country can least afford it. It is a lose-lose proposition for everybody not only in America but the world too.

Not only are we losing proceeds from the wages of production, but jobless people in the United States cannot afford to buy even the cheaply produced goods imported from nations employing slave labor in production. If we in the United States cannot afford to buy even cheaply produced goods we import daily form "sweatshop" and child labor" nations whose methods we decry, how long can those nations be economically viable? Domestically, incomes are shrinking, housing values are dropping, prices for basic commodities are skyrocketing, and consumers have hit an impenetrable spending wall. We are not spending because we have lost confidence; we have no *m-o-n-e-y.*

We, in the United States, are also importing supposedly, intellectually superior, well educated individuals from third world countries to develop all manner of new technology and hold technologically advanced jobs that *Americans are not educated enough to perform. What?* This creates a brain drain in developing countries which need their talent in order to grow and become economically viable so they can purchase what we produce. Genius exists in a certain percentage of our domestic population. Our domestic genius is undeveloped because of the lack of adequate emphasis on education in increasingly numerous disadvantaged communities and in inner cities. There are geniuses in those communities who, when given the chance, will most assuredly have answers to some of the problems we face. We exhibit the same attitude toward intellectual capacity that we exhibit toward the destruction of all-natural resources for economic gain. We treat intellect as if there was a never-ending source that we can purchase at will if we cannot develop domestic intellect through education. It seems corporate lobbyists whispering sexy, sweet-nothings in Congressional ears think it is easier, and cheaper to buy a foreign-born brain that it is to train our own. Segregation exists as much as it ever did but for different reasons. Instead of being based solely on race, the reason now more than ever, is clearly economic greed. We pay lip service to the idea of equality but put no monetary power behind making the concept a reality. That is why I maintain that instead of a democracy, we have an "ecotechnocracy."

Ecotechnocracy is my word and it means:

The economy built by corporate technology and governed by a supposedly democratic government (actually a representative republic). The reason failure is inevitable is because the politicians are not astute enough to understand technology and the way in which can be integrated into a democracy to make that democracy productive. Technology, by its very nature, cannot actually be managed by a democracy. It is counterintuitive. The American people have lost the power to control their government; and the government, if it ever had any, has lost the intellectual power to understand and control technology.

Our country is in the midst of a presidential election that may be the most important since the Founding Fathers formed the United States of America. While we have an African-American candidate in Barack Obama and had a woman candidate in Hilary Clinton, both brilliant and both a tribute to how far we have come in our thinking about the individual attributes and not the race or gender of the candidate, we still have far to go.

Just in 2007, I heard a person use the term "wigger," which I had never heard and I asked what it meant. I was told it meant "white nigger." This comment came from a person who probably does not consider themselves racist.

Racism is till a huge issue in 2008; it matters little how much we deny it, how much we try to gloss over it, ignore it, or claim significant progress in race relations. It still exists, and it is till a factor hurting our economy and our society. Polls, polls and more polls are being conducted by news organizations to ascertain whether race is a factor in the upcoming presidential election. The answer is a resounding yes. Political polls are much like marketing surveys that try do ascertain if *intent to but will result in an actual sale.* When polling individuals regarding the attitudes toward race in electing a candidate, many will answer that race doesn't matter; but when it comes time to vote, *does that attitude hold when the lever is pulled or the button is pushed?*

Not all men are created equal, that is the *ideal,* not the *reality,* and we do not yet have racial equality. We do *not* have gender equality. Both are a matter of justice, or lack thereof. It is incumbent upon each of us an individual to examine our thinking about the equality of all people and act accordingly. This is especially true regarding the education of our children who must carry our burdens into their future, and we all need to make sure racism is not part of the baggage we hand over to them. Another facet of the racism equation is that when racism is measured, it seems to be measured with regard to *white males*. Why is that? When compared to white males, all African-Americans are inferior? When compared to white males, all females are inferior? *When and how did the white male become the elite standard measure?* Observations of the state of America's economy and society today would indicate that if that is the measure, *somebody* made a *huge* mistake in *judgment*.

THE ISSUE OF THE FATHERLESS CHILD

Much has been made of the issue of the "fatherless black child." Bill Cosby has made his views abundantly clear about men who father children and do not perform their obligation as fathers. Barack Obama made it a central focus of his speeches, if not of his candidacy since he has only brought up the issue, not proposed any real solution. Maybe that is unfair to him because the solution is not a simple as throwing money at it. We can allocate more money for education, but education alone will not fix the problem. Blacks, however valiant their efforts cannot fix the issue alone. The fix will require everyone, black and white.

In the dismal days of slavery in the Old South, whole families were decimated by being torn apart in Africa and individual members chained and dragged to America like cattle. In most cases, if they lived, they never saw their family members again. That is just a historical fact.

Once the Africans were sold and put in place on plantations, if they ever managed have their own families with a wife and children, those individuals were often sold off and, once again, the family was decimated. There could never really be any sort of permanent family ties for people who could at any time be ripped away and sent to some unknown destination on another plantation. Even after slavery ended with Lincoln's Emancipation Proclamation, many of the African males had to find work, and that meant they had to leave any family they may have managed to have. By the time slavery ended several generations after Africans were first brought to this country, there would be no memory of the original family. After generations of families being torn apart by being auctioned off, there would be little reference for a strong family structure at all.

In the early days of freedom, there was little opportunity for former slaves. They could become sharecroppers but almost never land owners.

They could not vote; they could not participate in any government decision regarding their welfare; they were mistrusted, hated and often object of unjust and indiscriminate violence. Survival alone was hard enough; there was no opportunity to buy land, make a living, and suddenly create a solid family structure. Years of economic and social injustice have taken a terrible toll on the African-American community. *The history for black males has not been conducive to forming stable, economically viable family units.* I am not making excuses for black males. Things have changed for the better; and education, though not perfect, has had a positive effect; but given the legacy of years of economic and social injustice foisted on African-Americans, it is no wonder that parental responsibility for black males has been slow in coming. *Lest we forget, The Civil Rights Act of 1964 was only forty-five years ago.* There seems to be an attitude that once the Civil Rights Act was passed that was it, but the economic reality of unjust and unequal treatment persists to the detriment of real upward class mobility.

There are increasingly more black models now for young males to emulate, but it cannot be solely the responsibility of those individuals. The task is enormous, and it will take everyone working together for social and economic justice for all people for the United States to overcome the overwhelming issues we face trying to get our country back on track to prosperity and greatness. Once anyone, black or white, Asian or Hispanic, gets a taste of economic independence through education, resulting in social and economic justice, with the accumulation of wealth, a stable family structure will follow.

INSTITUTIONALIZED RACISM

Because personal bigotry has been practiced by so many for so long, racism has become institutionalized. Some realtors, no matter how much they deny the fact, continue to steer qualified African-American buyers away from predominantly "upscale white neighborhoods." Banks do not lend equally to blacks and whites. There is still wage disparity between working class whites and blacks. It was not until well after desegregation became law that affirmative action made some inroads into equal education, particularly on the college level. No thinking, observing individual can deny the public-school education is not on an even playing field for whites and blacks. Even with the progress in education with some resulting prosperity among African-Americans, our economy has begun to reap the *negative* consequences of institutionalized racism and discrimination in a big way.

The current crisis in our economy can be, at least partially, traced to criminally negligent racist lending behavior on the part of banks, appraisers in cahoots with banks, and realtors toward the African-American and other minority communities. Poor whites seeking a small piece of the American dream were also taken in by lenders who knew full well what they were doing when they agreed to lend to economically disadvantaged individuals who could not afford the homes they were buying. I have heard some say that it is the fault of the borrower for not understanding what they were signing. What the borrowers probably thought they were signing was their ticket to the American dream. The lenders knew what they were doing and the American dream has turned into the American nightmare for all of us even if we did not have a subprime loan.

Many minority-owned homes have gone into foreclosure, and many more will go into foreclosure before the full fallout of fraudulent lending has been realized. Because many of those homes were in black neighborhoods, entire communities will be dragged down. Cities containing those communities will be economically depleted, and the tax base supporting education and infrastructure will erode. In many instances, the resulting economic losses will be unrecoverable. Homes *will have* to be bought, in some cases renovated, in a time when there is *no credit* available from banks. The outlook is untenable. Banks have caused their own demise by engaging in risky lending policies in order to make a fast buck and, as a result, have lost *big* bucks.

Ironically, banks have systematically destroyed the very customer base they have relied upon for growth in previous decades. Banks were supported in their greed by the government, particularly Congress, when they passed banking legislation to enable the banking industry to engage in risky mortgage lending. The risky mortgage lending was compounded by unsound legislation on credit cards and "new and improved" bankruptcy laws.

The so -called 'mortgage meltdown' and the 'credit crisis' were brought on, at least partially, by institutionalized discrimination against the poor and economically disadvantaged. Our economy, based on consumer buying confidence, cannot survive without the support of people who work, pay taxes, buy houses, cars, and consumer goods.

Corporations who knowingly hire illegal workers, at low wages, are to blame for the erosion of the American way of life through the attrition of good paying jobs for our own citizens. Sending jobs to other countries is another form of racial and class discrimination allowing corporate exploitation of the poor, which is encouraged by our government, whether it is on the scare or federal level.

At a time when the "war of choice" in Iraq is waged by powerful ignorance and fought by the courageous hopeful, no one was watching as our national economy crumbled from the pillaging of "legalized greed" fully aided by corporate lobbyists and inept governance. This is the greatest realization of economic injustice waged on a population since the end of the Civil War.

LEARNING RACISM IN THE EARLY SCHOOL YEARS

A while back, I was on a medical appointment and was talking with the x-ray tech who happened to be a young black mother of two teens, a boy and a girl. Never one to miss a chance to discuss race relations, I asked her about her children and if they had faced racism. Her answer shocked me.

She recounted how, prior to her children attending public school, they had a totally mixed array of races of kids with which to play and socialize. She explained there had been blacks, whites, Asians, and Hispanic children in their neighborhood; and all the kids got along quite well. When her daughter attended the first grade, however, another little girl cold her one day she was "too dark" for her to play with.

The little girl who said the little black girl was too dark was Hispanic. The little Hispanic girl was also dark. They had been friends for the first few weeks of school; but when the mother, the x-ray tech, came to the school, someone pointed out that she was black. One of the children said, "Her Mama is black." Thus, they could no longer play with the child because she "as "too dark." The child had not changed color, the mother had not changed color, but the kids decided the child was too dark. Where did the kids gee the notion that, first, she, was too dark and, second, that they could not play with her because of it?

I asked her if her little girl was hurt by the comments and the treatment, and she said her daughter was tremendously hurt and did not understand.

The young black mother was surprised that the first hint of racism when her children went to school, and not only did it begin in school, it began with children who had been their friends prior to attending school. This incident would tend to lend credence to the notion that racism is learned, or born of environment, which-if it does not directly foster racism-does little to educate against it.

Kids are a cruel lot. I faced the brunt of being poor, being on meal tickets for school lunches when my father fell off a roof and broke his foot. He didn't work for a long time, and the kids made fun of me for getting "free lunches." This happened when I was in the fourth grade after the family moved co Charlottesville for better economic opportunities. Until then, I didn't know how poor we were because "in the country," we were all in the same miserable economic poverty boat. Like the little black girl, I didn't know I was different from anyone else until someone pointed out to me that I was poor. The hurt of others making fun of you as a child never, never goes away; and it shapes attitudes, personhood, achievement, and self-worth for as long as a person lives.

The horrible aftermath of other children making fun of a child is that the child may start to believe it is true; and without a strong family structure to work through it to overcome the psychological damage, the child is lost in a downward spiral of self-doubt, whether the discrimination was because of race, religion, economic status, or myriad other excuses for unjust treatment.

"IT FINALLY HAPPENED, WE'RE EQUAL!"

This editorial cartoon by Bob Englehart from 1995 says it better than I ever could. I clipped this cartoon, along with thousands of others I have collected over the years, because it spoke so clearly to the race situation at that time regarding affirmative action. The notion of affirmative action had everyone confused about exactly how racial equity should be achieved. We are still struggling in 2008.

This editorial cartoon was reprinted by written permission in 2008 from Mr. Bob Englehart personally, of the Hanford Courant. Permission was granted for one time use only to Carol R. Ellis for the purpose used in this book. It cannot be used for any other purpose and can nor be duplicated without express written consent of Bob Englehart.

TEN THINGS I KNOW FOR SURE

1. I do not believe in niggers, I believe in the human dignity of ALL people.
   Racism is evil and no one should use the racist word nigger.
2. Racism, as practiced by any race against any other race, is equally wrong.
3. Institutionalized racism-as practiced against African-Americans, Native Americans, and poor Americans of all colors-is entrenched in our social, financial, educational, and government systems in America.
4. As long as institutionalized racism exists, it will be difficult to eradicate it from individual thinking. And as long as racism exists in individual chinking, it will be difficult to eradicate it from the institutional practice of discrimination, resulting in social and economic injustice.
5. Racism is having a severe impact on d1e US economy, both domestically and internationally, by nor educating all children equally from the inner-city population to the rural poor population.
6. Racism is having a deeply deleterious impact on our ability to compete with global technology by stifling creativity.

7. Racism is limiting the thinking capacity and opportunities of our children to experience social diversity.

8. Racism, as practiced by blacks/blacks, white/blacks, blacks/white, is filling our prisons with unrealized, productive economic potential.

9. Racism has no positive upside; its practice serves none of us.

10. Racism is nor a "black-only problem," tr is a problem for all of us-it took years to institutionalize, and tr will cake years to undo, whether it is born of our very human nature or whether it is learned in an environment where the origins of its practice are not questioned and are little understood. Perhaps the practice of racism in the United States was born of the need to keep slaves as subservient, compliant, non-hostile, nonviolent free labor. That horrible time in our history is long over; but the attitudes of inferiority, as expressed by the very word "NIGGER" on the part of blacks and whites, remain as an archaic holdover that should no longer be tolerated by any race.

SUMMARY

Racism, in my belief, is somewhat akin to one of the seven Deadly Sins which are Anger, Lust, Envy, Gluttony, Slothfulness, Covetousness, and Pride. *Racism* too, is a moral failing which, not only destroys the spirit of the object of bigoted thinking, but the bigot themselves.

If an individual has a strong dislike, or hatred for a particular group of people, whether they are of a different race, religion, or sexual orientation, the attitude reveals more about the *hater,* than it reveals about the *object* of the hatred. Some with whom I have spoken do not know why they feel the way they do about certain groups of people. Those individuals do want to examine their beliefs and understand the importance of changing prejudiced attitudes because they realize the inherent negativity in bigotry. Others will remain intolerant, and infect their children with racist beliefs and bigoted practices, until they die. Some racists profess *religion* as a reason for their attitudes.

The practice of racism in our multi-cultural society keeps mankind from advancing economically, and spiritually. One's religion is not necessarily a factor in one's *spirituality,* which enables free and open practice of tolerance, and the belief in the higher nature, or goodness, of man. Religion confines thinking to a particular standard of beliefs, which in some cases, can be the antithesis of the free spirituality.

There are many who profess to be Christians and freely admit to being racists. It is impossible to be both.

Note *

When it became known that I was writing about racism some asked why I did not include all forms of bigoted behavior aimed at those who do not adhere to a particular predetermined ideal. My response is that what I have written is what I lived and what I know. I have many, many more stories from my life, and the lives of other white people, who came of age in the 1950's and l 960's, and earlier, who experienced much of the same injustice toward blacks by their families. Like me, they do not feel guilt, but rather a profound sadness with the practice of racism, and they are determined to bring positive change by not being racist themselves.

INDEX

9 798893 060430